Author's note

This is my story of School Refusal.

I am not a doctor or a child psychologist or a teacher. For the purposes of this book I am a mother.

I don't purport to be an expert. I am simply writing what I wish I knew at the beginning of this journey. This lonely, misunderstood, soul destroying journey.

I hope this book gives you some peace, some sense of not being alone, some information, some direction and most of all some hope.

There is hope! You will get through this and so will your child.

Copyright 2020

What is School Refusal?

School Refusal occurs when a child is unable to attend school regularly and without distress.

School Refusal is the Education Dept's dirty little secret. Its more common than you think, and it is on the increase.

It can happen at any age and can start slowly and build as time goes along or it can start in an instant, out of the blue. Sometimes there is an obvious preceding event and sometimes it is a mystery. Sometimes it comes and goes or appears to relapse.

Sometimes your child will be able to articulate exactly why they can't attend and sometimes they will just say "I don't know", "I just can't", "You wouldn't understand" or they will say nothing. They will just hide under the bed sheets and refuse to get up or get dressed. There may be tears, there may be shouting, there may be silence.

Whatever way it presents in your child, here you are.

What the hell just happened?

What do you mean you're not going to school? You have to go to school! Everyone goes to school! It's the law.

Then... You'll get into trouble if you don't go to school. I'll get into trouble if you don't go to school.

You just have to go to school!

I can't.......

You phone the school and tell them you're having trouble getting your child to school. They tell you that your child is legally required to attend school and that you should be firm with your child and if necessary they will meet you at the gate or at your car and they will help you encourage, force, shame or drag your child into the school grounds.

You do this for a few weeks or a few years until your child is physically big enough to resist. Or until you listen to your instincts which are telling you to protect your child and that this force does not feel ok.

As a parent you are caught between a rock and a hard place. Between your child who is begging you to help them feel safe and a system that is bearing down on you to force your child to attend school or face prosecution from the powers that be.

You need to go to work to earn money to live and you can't leave your child alone all day.

If you are lucky your child is attending a school that uses a trauma-informed, child-centred, collaborative, flexible and most importantly KIND approach.

If not read on…..

Take a deep breath

This is going to seem nearly impossible but try to take a deep breath.

Try not to panic and fell like your child's life is going to be totally ruined if you can't get them school in the next week

Look at your child with curiosity. What are they trying to tell you that they can't put into words? All Behaviour is a form of communication. Behind every negative behaviour there is a feeling and behind that feeling is an unmet need. What has made them feel unsafe to be in school?

Read that again

What has made them feel unsafe to be in school?

Are they being bullied and not supported properly by the adults around them?

Is there something going on at home that is making them worried about being away from you?

Is your child on the Autism spectrum and the school environment is overwhelming for them?

Do they have an undiagnosed learning difficulty or ADHD which is making the classroom impossible?

Whatever the reason, the solution is the same

Child-centred, trauma-informed, collaborative (school, parent, child,) wrap around scaffolding and a healthy pinch of kindness.

School Can't not School Won't

I like to refer to School Refusal as School Can't. If your child could go to school happily, they would. No child wants to worry their parents, or disappoint their teachers or risk getting in trouble. We all thrive when we feel safe and competent and make the people around us happy. It's human nature.

Once we change our perspective from the child being naughty or defiant to one of the child is struggling with something we can begin the helping and the healing.

Dr Ross Greene is a child psychologist and author who has written and spoken extensively on this subject. His books are definitely worth a read.

https://drrossgreene.com

If in doubt, choose kindness

There will be many times along this journey that you will feel conflicted. You've tried everything and you're exhausted, and you feel pressured by well-meaning family and friends to put your foot down!

It's easy for others who are looking from the outside in to pass judgment. Or maybe it is some advice from a professional or teacher that doesn't sit well with you but then you've run over it in your head so many times you tend to second guess yourself.

Sometimes you may feel frustrated with your child and can't understand what they need. Maybe if I get angry, they'll suddenly start going to school?

It doesn't work like that.

From my personal experience and from other parents on the other side of school refusal, I've asked "If you had to do this all over again would go harder or softer?"

They invariably say softer.

It's so easy to break trust and ruin a precious, precarious relationship with an anxious child and it is so difficult to repair.

If in doubt, choose kindness.

Attachment Theory Baby!

Google it.

 Secure Attachment is fundamental to us functioning confidently in the world.

Your child's healthy attachment to you is EVERYTHING. Guard it like you would a precious diamond. From this stable base your child will tentatively take their first steps away from you confident that you're there waiting if they need reassurance. Bit by bit the distances get bigger and longer.

Fear and anxiety and loss and trauma can damage a child's secure attachment.

The good news is it can be repaired.

If you can get yourself into a Circle of Security parenting course do it.

You're never too old to learn something new!

https://www.circleofsecurityinternational.com

https://www.verywellmind.com/what-is-attachment-theory-2795337

If it works do more, if it doesn't work stop doing it….

Sounds simple doesn't it? Sometimes we just need to remind ourselves not to over-complicate things.

Sometimes we put pressure on our kids to do things that aren't helping them because schools or social workers or whoever, says that's the way to do it.

A child-led trauma informed approach looks at what is working and heads in that direction. If something isn't working remove it or adjust it or add supports.

Some schools and teachers can be inflexible, authoritarian and lazy.

Other schools are forward thinking, flexible, solutions oriented and compassionate.

School refusal is complex and multi – causal. There is no easy one size fits all solution. It takes time and patience and curiosity to unpick what is going on for the child and find a solution that works.

As Einstein (maybe) once said "The definition of madness is doing the same thing over and over and expecting a different result"

If someone is not part of the solution, they are part of the problem (Build your team)

Your team will consist of any mix of school counsellors, teachers, well- being officers, child psychologists, educational psychologists, occupational therapists, mentors, family and friends.

Choose people who make this path easier, who like you and your child, who lighten your load not add to it. When something feels right it feels right, you know. Trust your instincts.

You are the expert of your child. Nobody knows them better than you.

This ties in with "If it works do more of it, if it's not working, stop".

Your team needs to be on your child's side. They need to be supportive, compassionate, wise, curious rather than judgemental preferably trauma-informed and most of all KIND.

It can take time to find the right team. Don't be afraid to say thanks but no thanks to people who aren't helping or don't feel right.

Join a Facebook peer support group for school refusal. There is a wealth of knowledge and non-judgemental support in these groups.

School Phobia/ School Refusal Australia (Facebook group)

Not fine in school: Family support for school attendance difficulties. (Facebook group)

There is more than one way to skin a cat....

Going to school every day all day and completing all work happily is Plan A.

But there is also Plan B, Plan C and Plan D or as many plans as your child needs.

Here are some suggestions for plans that might work for your child, ranging from minor tweaks to a major rethink of how education will look for your child.

Gradual re-exposure to school to build up resilience increasing slowly or at a pace your child can cope with.

Shorter days, increasing as your child's confidence grows

Varied/adjusted timetables

Varied and adjusted and supported curriculums

Home schooling

Distance education/ online learning

Unschooling for a period of time to allow trauma to be addressed

19

Remember there are many pathways to getting an Education. Attending mainstream school is one of them and great for most kids but definitely not for all. Not everyone wants to be a doctor or an Engineer. Some will be carpenters, bakers, hairdressers, artists, poets, musicians. Some will go to Uni straight out of school, some as mature-age students and some never at all. There is no one size fits all when it comes to life.

Safety first

Actually it's safety first, and second and third.

Something has happened that has made your child feel unsafe at school. It may be bullying, not understanding the work, not being able to reproduce the work in the way that the teacher or curriculum requires, it could be fear of being shamed or worry about being away from home, it could be that the school environment is too noisy and socially foreign and restrictive for a child who is not neuro-typical.

Until the issue of safety is addressed you risk re-traumatising your child and making things harder.

When our children feel heard, protected and supported and scaffolded they can then take the brave steps towards facing their fears and independence.

Our kids aren't bullet-proof, and we don't create resilience by boiling them in oil. Small supported steps led by the child create lasting confidence and intrinsic self-esteem. Allowing our kids to come back in to us for reassurance is the basis of Healthy Attachment.

As I wrote before secure, healthy attachment is fundamental to life.

Google Attachment Theory.

Inch by inch

Or as I prefer to call it...........Slow and steady wins the race.

It never pays to be in a hurry when dealing with School Refusal Behaviours.

Small steps in the right direction is progress. Standing still is ok. Take time with each step to allow your child to get used to the new normal. Sometimes it's tempting to push for the next level immediately after your child has a win.

Allow the child to take the lead, with you and your child's team supporting from behind. It's a real skill to be able to find the sweet spot between where your child is now and how big the next step can be without pushing them too far out of their comfort zone and then they panic and take two steps back.

So child-led, supported steps with time to consolidate the new normal creates lasting confidence and safety.

Another thing to remember is that if you allow your child to pull back when something gets too much it allows them to feel safe taking new steps. If they know they can come back if necessary, they are more likely to try new things.

Helping your child gain some sense of control over their journey encourages bravery.

Comparison is the Thief of Joy

You may find yourself grieving the loss of how things used to be, or how you thought they would be.

Social Media is full of photos of friends' kids first day of school, graduation, awards, celebrations, sports achievements, socialising the list goes on. It is a painful reminder of how simple your life used to be or the things you thought you would be celebrating with your child and now you're not or you're worried that it will not happen in the future.

It is soul destroying watching your child struggle. It's exhausting living with crushed hopes and dreams. We all want our children to have happy, normal (what's normal?) lives. We want them to walk or run through life without a care in the world sharing all the rites of passage with their peers.

When that dream gets ripped away or threatened it's extra hard celebrating all of your friends' children's achievements.

Comparison is truly the thief of joy.

Hide the posts. Celebrate your child's achievements even if they are not the same as almost everyone else.

We all walk through our lives on an individual timeline.

As a wise woman once told me … "Every dog has it's day!"

Get it in writing

School refusal is often complex and multi-causal and extremely difficult to negotiate. It doesn't fit well into the mainstream education model.

Teachers are overloaded and stressed, parents are often over-stressed and time poor, the education system is not particularly flexible and is more or less one size fits all. The mental health system is hugely underfunded and current view around School Refusal is that it is usually the parent at fault. Parents are viewed as indulgent, helicopter parents, enabling and projecting their own insecurities on their children.

I strongly disagree with this narrative.

Often Schools will have conversations over the phone or in face to face meetings. They don't put things in writing as a rule.

After every phone conversation shoot an email detailing what was said in the email by who.

After every face to face meeting write a summary and email to all attendees.

This will give you a paper trail.

You may need it.

What's in an ILP

An Individual Learning Plan or IEP, Individual Education Plan or AIP, Attendance Improvement Plan are wonderful tools. For the purpose of this chapter we will refer to them all as ILPs.

Whatever your school calls it, it needs to be done right.

It can set the framework for supporting and scaffolding your child while they are at school or transitioning back into school.

It is a COLLABORTIVE document consisting of agreements between the child, the school, the parents and possibly outside support people including OTs, speech pathologists, psychologists, advocates or anyone who is involved in your child's well-being.

These plans let everyone know what is expected of them and what they can reasonably expect in return.

A good ILP is child-centred, trauma-informed and strengths-based. It is important we listen to the child, help the child to identify areas of struggle and work out ways to either remove the stressor or support the child through the deficit.

Reasonable adjustments are modifications that are individually tailored to your child's needs and can include, use of technology to assist learning, modified timetables, timeout plans, learning supports, speech recognition technology, uniform modifications, identification of safe people or safe rooms where children can go when it is too much. The possibilities are limitless.

An ILP is a working document. That means it can and should be regularly revisited and adjusted as the needs of the child change or increase or decrease.
A good rule of thumb is to review after the 1st month and then after that review each term of as required.

Revisiting the ILP allows everyone to have a look at what is working and what isn't working and tweak accordingly.

Scaffold, support and notice the small things

I love the imagery created by the word scaffolding. It is a protective framework that ensures the safety of whatever is inside until what is inside is strong and stable enough to remove the scaffolding and stand alone. It is not designed to be there forever.

Picture a young, thin, bendy tree sapling. It is planted in the ground and stakes are placed around and the young sapling is watered and fed until its trunk is strong and straight enough to stand without the props holding it up.

In some cases there may be supports needed that will not be able to be removed. The support will allow access to learning. it won't make the disability go away, but it will allow the child to function and engage in a way that maximises potential and live life the best they can.

Nobody ever did better at something because someone shamed them or threatened them or pointed out how wrong they did it. That's not getting the best out of children its ruling by fear being shamed or belittled.

When we notice the small things a child is doing right, and we comment on it and its true the child is empowered to do more that. The praise we give to kids about things they do well becomes their internal dialogue.

Think about it. We all have things in our heads that people have said to us. Good things and bad things. Words are powerful and become our internal voices. Let that be "I am good at things" "I tried really hard and someone noticed".

It's not rocket science. Kindness and praise are never ever wasted.

No threat is scarier than school

No punishment is worse than going to school
No bribe is tempting enough to get them attending happily
No amount of begging will make them feel guilty enough to go

Fear is a great motivator

If your child only feels safe at home or feels unsafe in school then no amount of threatening, rewarding or cajoling will work for any period of time.

The trick is to unpick what is making them feel unsafe and either introduce supports or remove stressors.

Once your child feels safe and supported and heard they can take the first brave step towards going to school.

If we can set our children up to do things because they are intrinsically important to them, they will be less likely to seek extrinsic validation as they grow older.

Lasting change that matches a child's value system is much healthier than responding to an outside stimulus of either threat or reward.

When a child feels safe, they will move towards growth.
Safety is expansive and makes a person's world larger.
Fear causes the world to contract and become smaller.

Meet your child where they're at

Perhaps one of the hardest things to do in this School Refusal journey is letting go of how you think your child should behave, what you think your child should be able to achieve, what they used to be able to do, what all of their friends seem to be doing, what you had hoped they'd do and how you planned your future as a parent.

When our children are struggling with something and not feeling they are coping, what they need to hear from us is the same thing we as adults need to hear from others around us.

We don't want people saying to ignore how we feel and "just do it", we don't want people to say "wow, you're making my life really difficult by feeling this way", or "if you could just try a bit harder I'm sure you'll be different" or " I really don't like you when you aren't doing all the things I really want you to do".

What we need to hear when we are feeling really afraid and overwhelmed and like we have failed ourselves and our families, is that it is ok. That we are ok just as we are, that the person sitting in front of us will carry the load for a bit and loves us just as we are and has faith that we will work out a way to move forward in a time and manner that is ok for us. We need that person to hold space for us, to ride the wave with us and ask us what we need from them right in this moment and to honour that wish.

It's really hard to do that when we see our children struggling. Their anxiety becomes our anxiety and away we go in that cycle.

I found this podcast really helpful in helping me accept my child right where he was at. Dr Shefali Tsabary on conscious parenting.

https://podcasts.apple.com/au/podcast/oprahs-supersoul-conversations/id1264843400?i=1000411005760

https://youtu.be/hBeJ6nUOHL8

Put on your own Oxygen Mask

Airlines know it. They tell us before every flight. In case of emergency put your own mask on before trying to save your children. If we can't breathe, we can't help anyone around us.

Self-care is really important. Self-care isn't always a massage and a three week holiday in the Bahamas. Sometimes self-care looks like saying no to something you don't have the energy to do, or that makes you feel sad. Self-care can be not having people in your life who don't support you. It can be deciding that you are not going to justify yourself or your child to people who are judgemental and unhelpful and make you feel bad.

School refusal is marathon not a sprint, and sometimes is a roller coaster marathon. You need to pace yourself, nurture yourself and take time to fill your cup and not feel one bit of guilt about doing that.

So have that bath, do that yoga class, binge a Netflix series, walk the dog, call an old friend do whatever it is that fills you cup.

Your child is more than a grade

Education is one part of a child's life. As parents we manage our children's emotional, physical, spiritual and mental development. It is a gradual process of guiding and letting go. As our children grow and develop our influence decreases and their autonomy over their life choices increases.

Going to school is one part of a complex machine. For many children going to school is an accepted part of life. Some thrive in the environment, some tolerate it and for some it is extremely stressful.

For some the academic model fits like a glove. Their life paths are clear and logical and achieving good grades comes naturally and gives them enormous joy.

For other children its sport, or music or art or technology.

Grades are not the only measurement for success.

Learning doesn't simply stop when we turn 22. We are all life-long learners, whether it be in a university setting, or taking an art class or learning new skills on a job. There are many pathways to success and that looks different to each one of us.

On Children
Khalil Gibran - 1883-1931

Your children are not your children.

They are the sons and daughters of Life's longing for itself.

They come through you but not from you,

And though they are with you yet they belong not to you.

You may give them your love but not your thoughts,

For they have their own thoughts.

You may house their bodies but not their souls,

For their souls dwell in the house of tomorrow, which you cannot visit, not even in your dreams.

You may strive to be like them, but seek not to make them like you.

For life goes not backward nor tarries with yesterday.

You are the bows from which your children as living arrows are sent forth.

The archer sees the mark upon the path of the infinite, and He bends you with His might that His arrows may go swift and far.

Let your bending in the archer's hand be for gladness;

For even as He loves the arrow that flies, so He loves also the bow that is stable.

www.ingramcontent.com/pod-product-compliance
Lightning Source LLC
Chambersburg PA
CBHW031248130726
47988CB00008B/3292